Nina Dont

sky full of scars

Bibliografische Information der Deutschen Nationalbibliothek: Die Deutsche Nationalbibliothek verzeichnet diese Publikation in der Deutschen Nationalbibliografie; detaillierte bibliografische Daten sind im Internet über dnb.dnb.de abrufbar.

Cover: Nina Dont

Verlag: BoD · Books on Demand GmbH, In de Tarpen 42, 22848 Norderstedt

Druck: Libri Plureos GmbH, Friedensallee 273, 22763 Hamburg

ISBN: 978-3-7693-0202-8

sky full
of scars

nina dont

for the ones who refuse to hate their scars
and the ones
who categorize their life in parts

friendship

[frend-ship]

noun
1 the state of being a friend; association as friends:

to value a person's friendship.

2 a friendly relation or intimacy.

3 friendly feeling or disposition.

nothing has changed
my friends still hang out without me

i'm sad
and lonely
and depressed

my mind is a scary place

and what's left of my sanity
can be found in my words

we make plans
you cancel them
we make new plans
and you cancel them
we make a lot of plans
and you cancel all of them

how am i not seeing a pattern?
or do is see it and refuse to notice?
or do i care and yet don't want to give up?

we make plans and you cancel them

and i still
try to stay in your life
try to keep you relevant in mine
try to hold on to a friendship build on breaking
grounds

we make plans and you cancel them

am i punishing myself just to feel something?

am i making a fool of myself?

we make plans and you

d i d n ' t

cancel them

　　y e t

but i know you will

and still

i will make new ones with you

i want to be

c h o s e n

for a change

i want to feel like i belong

like someone cares

like i make a difference in someone's life

so i'm just waiting here

yesterday
you touched my face
it's been too long i hold onto my grace

one year ago
you held me tight
whispered
let's meet again i'll make this right

three years before that
we said goodbye
snug embrace
and all i did was cry
we will never lose touch a promise i believed

write me a word

or

write me a paragraph

the sight of your name

h u r t s

just the same

your friendship feels like

two weeks of rain in july

i still have the polaroid

of you kissing my cheek

should i throw it out?

or should i keep it for the sake of feeling my heart
combust every time i look at it

just to know

that i'm still able to feel something?

i'm always the odd one out

the one

that has to fall behind

when the sidewalk narrows

the one

you don't cancel your plans for

and yet the one plans always get cancelled on

the one that sometimes simply gets forgotten

while i'm the one

that gives you all their attention

the one

that crosses the sea for you

the one

that sometimes cries on the bathroom floor

when the weight of being forgotten gets too much

i don't care

but i do

a disappointed and brokenhearted girl

that just wants to be on the inside for once

i don't care

but i do

i want to be the first choice for once

lovelorn

describes the sadness

of unrequited love

but

is there also a word that describes

the unbearable sadness

of unrequited friendship?

or

does everyone else have a best friend that just feels
the same for them?

trapped in a crystal ball

i'm inside
looking out
i'm trapped
with no way around

they're laughing
having fun
they don't see me
or this gun

i think about ending it
i'm so alone
they were my friends
but threw the first stone

i cry and scream
they can't hear me
did i do something wrong?
do the now fear me?

i'm inside
looking out
these are the friends
i'm crying about

i look at the gun
heavy in my hand
would you cry for me?
would you weep, old friend?

it's tearing me apart
that we don't speak
i hate the fact
i wasn't yours to keep

i chose you

i choose you

hours in the car just

to see you for a few minutes

spending the weekend listening to your stories

it's one sided

but i still choose you

o how i hated high school and
all the mean girls
disguised as friends
and how i was always alone on the weekends
i thought when you're thirty
the mean girls would be nice
seems like
i just got burned twice

i can fill up all the journals

within my reach

with encouraging lines

about how they don't deserve me

but at the end of the day

i will be back

on their doorstep

begging them to let me in

because

i just want to feel seen

deep down

i know i should be grateful

for even the smallest crumbs

you hand me

i should just be happy and thankful

for the friendship

you're willing to give

but

there's also a part of me

that's just aching for more

you mourn her

and we both know

you feel like

you just lost the wrong friend

trusted me with your secret

said *no one knows*

and i proudly kept it

appreciating you shared something with me

so valuable to you

shadows followed

my thoughts

hung to my lips

as i whispered

am i nothing more to you?

lovers

impossible

so i settled on being friends

slipping out of contact

was a slow process

could never

     pinpoint

the moment we weren't friends anymore

one day

we just weren't

sometimes i get the urge to call you but i seem

to have lost your number

i consider visiting the house you last lived in

see if your parents still know my name and if

your brother is still in love with me

it's been years

so they probably don't

what a trick life plays on you:

giving you a person you shared everything with and

then taking them away

you were my best friend

now you're a person whose laugh i find annoying

i'm a pick me girl

i want you to pick me

to choose me

i want to be on your mind

to be the only one

the first one

the only one

i'm begging you to pick me

just this once

pick me

craving the water

in the middle of a dry spell

raising high hopes

until we both fell

abandoned

like the bushes on the side of the road

left me stranded

put my measly life on hold

being your friend involves:

- being there for you

- making you the main character in my life

- stepping down when you need someone else

- drop everything when you call

- plan my life around your needs

this is *just* a checklist i need to keep

never the first choice

always the burden

promises were made

but colors they fade

you left me for a reason

changing like the season

now i'm screaming at the moon

crying to be done soon

ice cream

in the middle of the night

conversations

about this not feeling right

riding shotgun with you

for the rest of my life

instead

getting stabbed to death

by your invisible knife

whispering secrets

guarded by our hands

talking on the phone

late at night

travelling the world together

being annoyingly cute in front of everyone

feeling at home in each other's eyes

- i wonder what it feels like to have a best
  friend

sharing honesty

talking while you listen

validating my words

feeling seen

and understood

and honored by your advice

smiling

i pay and leave the taxi

the smell of popcorn

and black and white movies on a bulky tv

childhood memories of just you and me

falling asleep next to each other

whispering because of your mother

transport me back

i plead with tears in my eyes

for i long to stay in simpler times

like water running through my fingers

i slowly felt you fading away

i couldn't hold on to you

now i know you wouldn't want me to

i'm scared one day you'll ask me to marry you

because how should i ever tell you

that i have no one to be my bridesmaid

i just need

s o m e *o n e*

who cares

love

[luhv]

noun
1 a strong feeling of
warm personal attachment or
deep affection, such as for a parent, child, friend, or
pet.

2 a profoundly tender, passionate affection, often
mingled with sexual desire, for another person.

3 ...

i
was the beginning of summer
&
you
were our end

we broke up

fairytale beginning

ending up in flames

fantasizing about a future

breaking all the same

for me it was it

for you maybe just a game

in another life

maybe we'll meet again

maybe we won't

just know

i love you

even when i don't

once i saw your face in every stranger

now i only see a stranger in your eyes

the baggage claim stopped an hour ago
with me still on it
it's getting late
it's getting dark
i'm still waiting
come find me and disembark

i have this feeling you will not come

it's hard living through mondays for the rest of
eternity

when i once knew the

    brightest

    funniest

    loveliest

saturdays with you

screaming into my pillow
i can't see clearly
it's you i want to follow
to just hold you near me

breaking me was always your point
crying *i deserve it*
leaving my heart disjoint
hoping <u>she</u> was worth it

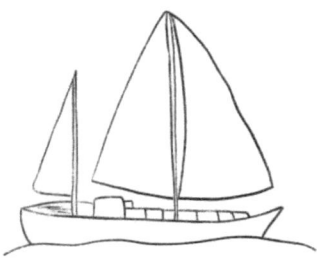

sabotaging myself to the point where

i'm no longer happy

instead doubting everything around me

bury myself in thoughts of sorrow

leaving no room to breathe

white sails vast ship

and let myself sink beneath

spring

when we met

flowers grew

easiness came

we fell in love

in the heat of the summer

swore to be forever

until fall washed the warmth away

led our love astray

so by winter

under the snows heavy composition

my body fell into submission

you were a thunderstorm
crashing into my life
with the full force that you are
the life of every party
always the first to dance and the last one to leave
your aura radiant in the brightest colors
the most welcoming tones
never to be defeated

but ...
she broke you

you're still you
but different

still a thunderstorm
but softer
still the party
but shorter
still radiant
but in pastels

eyes restless as if they're searching

for something greater

always wandering around and mumbling that you
hate her

nonetheless

i still love you

maybe even more

shivers ran down my spine

when you finally whispered the words i

desperately

    d e s p e r a t e l y

wanted to hear

only to realize

they were what i wanted

but not what i needed

i'm falling

-    for you
-    in love
-    for your lies
-    out of love

you bought a centerpiece

but that doesn't fix a broken home

maybe i was just the side plot in your story

and i was never meant to be there for the happy end

it's october now

april seems so long ago

and yet no time has passed

since you left me aghast

words can't possibly describe how much i love you

you're the first and last thought on my mind

every little part
of my body and soul belongs to you

and yet
      and yet

all the poems i write
i write about her

listening to lana because of you

i feel her *heart* a c h e

and i wonder if you do

too

fiercely in love

yet vomiting only depressing words on paper

i miss you

> in bed playing keyboard on my ribs on
> a sunday morning in the middle of
> november

i miss you

> telling me daily i'm the most beautiful
> woman you have ever seen

i miss you

> kissing me on every red light we
> stopped at so it became a tradition

i miss you

> and even the stupid fights leading to
> our breakup

i miss you

> but i'm wise enough to acknowledge
> the ending

do i ever cross your mind?

do you

  smile

  light up

  get excited

when you think about me?

do you remember my scent

my warm touch

or my face blush?

do you recall us lying on the concrete gazing at the
stars

and me at you?

do you remember reading my words

and realizing the muse?

and if you don't

please don't tell me

i'm doing just fine in my delusion

i never knew you felt like this

i thought i made it obvious

how?

staring and caring

i guess i never realized …

i know

you were too busy
with her

when you're next to me

and our bodies touch

i fall asleep easily

i feel your breath in my neck

and i cannot be happier

because it means you're there

but when you're not

my mind can't calm down

and i can't find peace

i miss you next to me

you snoring next to me is my level of comfort

you never told me you loved me

but the flowers did
and the coffee and the homemade cakes
the silent talks
the bright smiles
and the future dreams

i told you a million times
you never really listened

she's five foot six and feisty

i really hope she likes me

oh happy day

kissing burgundy lips

sunset ember gleaming in our bonfire hearts

while your sun kissed hair reflects golden on my
skin

and the

sage green hope of optimism hanging from the walls

cerulean eyes, promising and wide like the ocean

sing to me with your fingertips tracing my lavender
scars

it's true

i see these colors because of you

decorating time in my favorite sounds of you

blue moon in august

you're admiring her

pretty captivating

i nod

she seems so close and yet out of reach

i nod

she is the prettiest thing I've ever seen

i nod

still gazing at you

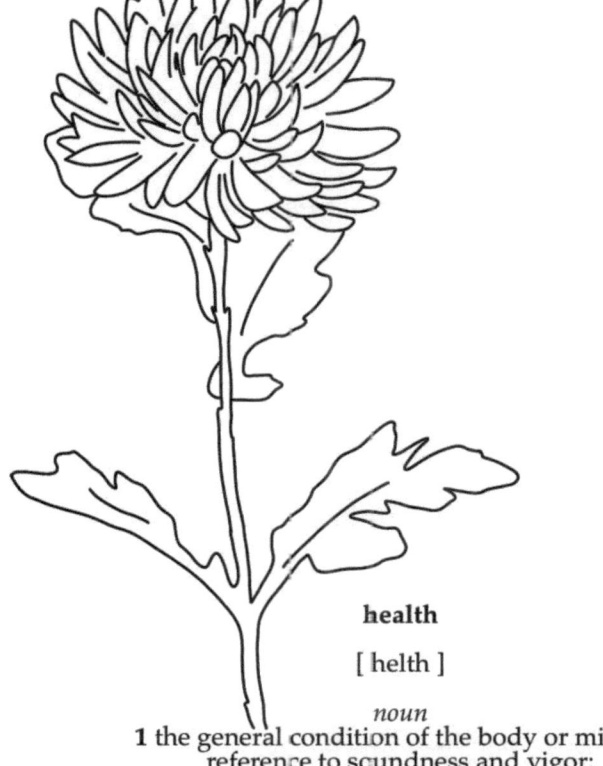

health

[helth]

noun

1 the general condition of the body or mind with reference to soundness and vigor:

good health;
poor health.

2 soundness of body or mind; freedom from disease or ailment:

to have one's health;
to lose one's health.

for the next year

i'm not 34

i'm still 33

on my next birthday i will turn 35, i promise

but please: let me be 33 for just one more year

i was 33 once

but i barely lived that year

i don't care for 34, i care for 33

but it's poisoned with bad memories and fluorescent light

so let me be 33 for one year longer so i can fill it up with

good memories until i only think about that year fondly

-   cancer took so much from me, please let me have this

how are you?

abandoned by my health and
just barely hanging on
good. and you?

old people telling me

to value my youth

    and *h e a l t h*

as if young people don't get cancer

putting on a mask

because i need to be the brave one

    the fun one

    the strong one

i put up a charade

so you can cry, and scream and hate everything

and i get to cuddle you until you fall asleep

only then will i allow myself to cry, too

i'll always be there for you

sometimes it takes a life-threatening illness to realize
that this is nothing more than a phrase

my fear invited you in

forcing me to victory

in a battle

i could barely win

and yet i conquered what was the fight of my life

trying to hide i'm shattered

into a million little parts
and dying of a broken heart

- it's all happening for a reason

- trust the universe

- maybe that's god's plan

- everything will be okay

- at least you lost some weight

- fucked up things you should never say to a cancer patient

clouds in the shape of
long lost loved ones
passing by
as i lay in my grave
waiting to die

mourning those who went before me
longing for a reunion sincerely
hoping for the cold soil beneath me
to suck me in completely

with my slowly dying heartbeat
i will tranquillize
farewell bittersweet

the moon is wailing to hold on
but i'm finally free
from this g o d f o r s a k e n misery

not sentimental

just mental

tiresome fights

with invisible ghosts

falling

and hanging on to bedposts

screaming voices in my head

we need therapy

but feels like a threat

brush strokes on bald skin

my life in ruins

no-win

clear to me

and plain to see

you liked me better when i was sick

craved your attention

i was your hyper fixation

but then you

left me hanging moved on to someone new

i'm the burden you outgrew

time will heal all wounds

not this one though

this one will stay forever

for someone terrified of death

i find myself daydreaming about it quite often

my body is full of scars

from times i had to be braver than i wanted to be

i wear them proud

as a sign of my resilience

i lie to myself all the time
but my favorite one is

everything will be alright

sometimes

when i charge my crystals in the moonlight

i make myself comfortable next to them

because

sometimes

i too need charging

i'm not your prime example

i'm not your cautionary tale

i'm openly vulnerable for growing purposes

even when it's scary

even when i'm horrified

i'm more than this tragedy

it's not all i am

i was healthy before

and i sure as hell will be healthy again

one threat will not define me

for the rest of my life

only the scars on my body will tell the tale of

how.

i.

s u r v i v e d.

horrible things i've seen

dire things i've felt

and a milliard times i wanted to die

but now

my scans are clean

congratulations are heartfelt

and i waved the shadows goodbye

The End

Part II

Thanks to …

… Luisa (@nichtspoilerfrei) for proofreading and
always being the one to hype me and my writing up.
Thank you for being there for me.

… my friends and family, for making my life worth
living.

About the author

Nina Dont lives with her family near Frankfurt in Germany. She writes novels and short stories and sometimes poetry.

Contact her via E-Mail (ninadont@gmx.de) or Instagram (@ninasbooktalk) or check out her website (www.ninadont.de) for further information.

Definitions:

https://www.dictionary.com/